Garfield
The Reluctant
Romeo

JIM DAVIS

D1350960

RAVETTE BOOKS

First published by
Ravette Books Limited 1992
Reprinted 1992

Printed and bound in Great Britain
for Ravette Books Limited,
3 Glenside Estate, Star Road, Partridge Green,
Horsham, West Sussex RH13 8RA
An Egmont Company
by Cox & Wyman Ltd, Reading

ISBN 1 85304 391 5

GARFIELD, WE'RE ON A DIET. LEAVE ODIE'S FOOD ALONE!

© 1990 United Feature Syndicate, Inc.

JIM DAVIS   4-12

© 1990 United Feature Syndicate, inc.

© 1990 United Feature Syndicate, Inc.

GARFIELD, YOU'RE CARRYING THIS BANANA THING TOO FAR!

THMILE WHEN YOU THAY THAT!

JIM DAVIS 5-18

JIM DAVIS 6-15

I AM PERSONALLY LOOKING FORWARD TO COLDER WEATHER

JIM DAVIS   6-20

© 1990 United Feature Syndicate, inc.

© 1990 United Feature Syndicate, Inc.

WAS THAT AN ECLIPSE?

© 1990 United Feature Syndicate, Inc.

JIM DAVIS 7-4

OH, IT WAS JUST GARFIELD WALKING PAST THE WINDOW

SHADDUP

IT'S IMPOSSIBLE NOT TO ENJOY THE PLAYFUL NATURE OF A CAT

JIM DAVIS 7-5

HEY, GARFIELD. LET'S HAVE SOME FUN!

© 1990 United Feature Syndicate, Inc.

DO YOU HAVE AN APPOINTMENT?

THE SECRET TO CATCHING BIRDS IS PATIENCE

© 1990 United Feature Syndicate, Inc.

UH... GARFIELD

SHHH!

JIM DAVIS 7-7

CLICK

JIM DAVIS 7-12

© 1990 United Feature Syndicate, Inc.

GARFIELD! WHAT HAVE YOU BEEN UP TO?!

WHAT MAKES YOU THINK I'VE BEEN UP TO SOMETHING?

BEWARE OF DOG

WHAT THE...?

MOTH ON A WINDSHIELD

JIM DAVIS 8-8

© 1990 United Feature Syndicate, Inc.

OTHER GARFIELD BOOKS IN THIS SERIES

LANDSCAPE SERIES

COLOUR TREASURIES

COLOUR TV SPECIALS

Here Comes Garfield	£2.95
Garfield On The Town	£2.95
Garfield In The Rough	£2.95
Garfield In Disguise	£2.95
Garfield In Paradise	£2.95
Garfield Goes To Hollywood	£2.95
A Garfield Christmas	£2.95
Garfield's Thanksgiving	£2.95
Garfield's Feline Fantasies	£2.95
Garfield Gets A Life	£2.95
Garfield A Weekend Away	£4.95
Garfield Book Of Cat Names	£2.50
Garfield Best Ever	£4.95
Garfield The Easter Bunny?	£3.95
Garfield How To Party	£3.95
Garfield Selection	£5.95
Garfield His 9 Lives	£5.95
Garfield Diet Book	£4.95
Garfield Exercise Book	£4.95
Garfield Book Of Love	£5.95

All these books are available at your local bookshop or newsagent, or can be ordered direct from the publisher. Just tick the titles you require and fill in the form below. Prices and availability subject to change without notice.

Ravette Books Limited, 3 Glenside Estate, Star Road, Partridge Green, Horsham, West Sussex RH13 8RA.

Please send a cheque or postal order and allow the following for postage and packing. UK: Pocket-books—45p for one book, 20p for a second book and 16p for each additional book. Landscape Series—50p for one book plus 30p for each additional book. TV Specials and Cat Names—45p for one book plus 30p for each additional book. Other titles—85p for one book plus 50p for each additional book ordered.

Name ....

Address ....

....